# EQUIPPED FOR GLORY

# GLORY

## UNDERSTANDING THE FIVE-FOLD GRACES

**Ian Carroll**

Equipped for Glory

Understanding the Five-Fold

© 2019 Ian Carroll

Building Contenders

Oak Park, Il, 60304 USA

ian@buildingcontenders.com

ISBN: 978-0-9982644-2-4

# TABLE OF CONTENTS

# INTRODUCTION

What's all the fuss about the five-fold gifts?

How do they operate?

Why is everyone calling themselves an apostle these days?

How do I know if I'm five-fold?

If I'm five-fold, how do I operate in my church?

Good questions. And it can be hard to find good answers. In fact, I've been asked these and related questions so often, I decided it was time I gathered some material together to help us recognize and use the five-fold gifts.

If you are unfamiliar with the five-fold gifts, I hope that these pages will help you understand them. If you've heard a lot about the gifts, I hope you'll be inspired to consider whether you've been understanding them correctly.

I would add that it is totally possible for Godly men and women to come to differing conclusions about the same topic. It is not only possible, it is healthy. These are some of my thoughts and beliefs, but they are not supposed to end a conversation, my hope is that they add to it.

And you'll find more Q & A at the end because it's at least as important to keep asking questions as it is to find answers.

So…are you ready to have some thinking on the five-fold challenged?

# 1: CHANGE YOUR MIND

If I started this book by saying, "repent!" you might stop reading. So I won't. I'll start by saying: It's all about the Kingdom. That sounds better, right?

Yet Scripture tells us to repent for the Kingdom is at hand. It doesn't say "hold more meetings for the Kingdom is at hand." If we're not seeing enough Kingdom, the problem is not with the King; the King is still on the throne.

Since that's the case, the problem must be with our thinking—we've got to change the way we think. That's what repentance is. So yes, I am saying we need to repent; we need to literally change our minds. When we do, we will see more Kingdom come.

Admittedly, it's hard to change how you think if you think you're right. I once attended a small meeting with a mighty man of God, the Christian academic, C. Peter Wagner. I was stunned when he said, "You know, I don't believe some of what I've written over the years anymore." What? Entire movements and schools have been created based around what this man taught. But he's an academic, and he understands that learning is a journey; some of what we believed ten years ago shouldn't be what we believe today.

Unfortunately, the Church often gets stuck on old beliefs, which we then carve into dogma. Instead, we should be adjusting and changing our thinking when we gain new knowledge and revelation.

Look at how we think of ourselves. I run some Schools of Emerging Apostles. Someone warned me, "Hey, you might inflate people's egos."

Hmmm. Let's read a passage from the Bible:

> By the grace given me I say to every one of you: Do not think of yourself more highly than you ought, but rather think of yourself with sober judgment, in accordance with the faith God has distributed to each of you (Romans 12:3: NIV).

People read that and assume it means we're not supposed to be building up people's egos because we're not supposed to think more highly of ourselves than we ought. Instead, I'd like to suggest that we don't think of ourselves the way our heavenly Father thinks of us. What father or mother tells their child, "I don't want you to be too successful? I think you're pretty average—please stay that way for your own good." Who says that to their children?

The problem isn't thinking too highly of ourselves. The problem is: can you think highly *enough* of yourself? Can you think highly enough of yourself to say, "I am a child of God. I am loved. I was bought with a price. I am blessed when I come in, I am blessed when I go out. I am the head, not the tail." That's what Scripture tells us to think. Jesus came that you would have a life and that you would have it in abundance—not in mediocrity. Jesus is a threat to our mediocrity.

We need to change our understanding of how the five-fold works so that we can raise up world-changers. That's my mission in life: to raise up world-changers.

I know from experience that we can spend a lot of time not changing anything at all. I was once part of a movement. Well, we called ourselves a movement until we stopped moving and we became an association. This association had created a whole slew of definitions about the five-fold based on error.

One chunk of that dogma was the idea of the Kingdom as "now-and-not-yet." In other words, the Kingdom is here, but it's also not yet—there will a day when it will be fully manifest. And when some people started to challenge the "not yet," other people started to reinforce the old dogma. Trying to fit an old belief system from the fifties into the current paradigm was trying to fit a square peg into a round hole.

What if you've been operating with the wrong idea of the five-fold? Are you willing to correct any old or wrong thinking? That happens to be one of the roles of the five-fold: to bring correction.

## GETTING AN ADJUSTMENT

> And He gave some [as] apostles, and some [as] prophets, and some [as] evangelists, and some [as] pastors and teachers, for the equipping of the saints for the work of service, to the building up of the body of Christ; until we all attain to the unity of the faith, and of the knowledge of the Son of God, to a mature man, to the measure of the stature which belongs to the fullness of Christ (Ephesians 4:11-12 NASB).

Ephesians 4 describes the role of the five-fold as equipping the saints to minister. The word translated here as equipping comes from a Greek medical term that means to reset or adjust a bone. So, equipping is about resetting, not just teaching. Have you ever had a bone reset without anesthesia? I've broken my nose a couple of times. Resetting it was painful. Well, equipping can be painful, too. Resetting bones may not be a pain-free experience and changing your beliefs may not be either. But Jesus is absolutely clear: The Kingdom is at hand. And He prefaced this by saying, "Repent." Are we up for repenting? For changing our minds?

Here's a prayer for just that. If possible, say it aloud with one hand on your head, and one hand on your heart:

> Jesus, I give you permission to change my head and to change my heart. This prayer is for me. It's not for my spouse or my child or my pastor. This is for me. So, do what you need to do. Amen.

It's vital to understand that this prayer is for yourself. Not for your pastor, your leader, your husband, or your wife. Not for the person you want to adjust! This prayer is not to get another person to repent. Matthew 3:2 says "Repent, for the Kingdom of heaven is at hand" (NASB). We each do this for ourselves; we are the ones responsible for changing our minds.

That's the starting point for changing the world. I mentioned that my mission in life is to raise up world-changers, and part of that mission is to address a glaring problem in the Church: a problem with authority.

# 2: AUTHORITY

People don't like authority. They ask: "Why can't we all be the same?" Sorry: God isn't a communist. He has *not* made us all the same. The Kingdom is not a round table. Grace is extended the same, but favor is different.

We might wonder, "Why do other people have great favor in their lives, and I don't?" And then, to make up for our perceived lack, we try to remove *all* favor: "If I can't have it, no one can." Or simply, "It doesn't exist." Sadly, many in the Church have done this for just about everything—favor, healing, miracles. You name it, we tend to get small-minded about it if we don't experience it for ourselves.

So, we have these extremes: either we all have equal X, Y, & Z or none of us have X, Y, & Z. Neither mindset sounds really healthy, does it? Such thinking results in some five-fold teachings that basically say: "There, there. We're all in this together, and we're all five-fold." No, not everything is five-fold. Saying so removes authority from the equation.

The solution to this issue is authority. And the current problem is that the Church is not walking in the authority it should be walking in. Jesus said, "All authority is given to me. Now go." Jesus transferred authority to us. And yet we can't even cure a headache. There is a disconnect here somewhere.

When John Wimber, founder of the Vineyard church, was praying for a thousand people and not seeing anybody healed, he went to the Lord and asked, "God, why am I not seeing anybody healed?" And he felt the Lord say to him, "The problem isn't on my end." Ouch. But if you say that in churches, people will automatically start to retort, "If someone doesn't get healed, are you saying it's their fault?" No. I'm saying it's *ours*. It is *our* responsibility to walk in a greater measure of signs and wonders than we have ever experienced before. That's our responsibility. Repent—change your mind—for the Kingdom is at hand.

If the problem is authority, we should understand what authority means. Let's start by looking at two Greek words: *exousia* and *dunamis*. They both mean power, though *exousia* also means authority.

*Dunamis* is the oomph we all love. An example of *dunamis* is when the Holy Spirit shows up, and people shake and fall down, and the demonic is broken off their lives, and they stand up restored. I love *dunamis*. This is what Jesus mentions in Mark 9:29, referring to the power to cast out a demon.

*Exousia* is power and authority—governmental and/or spiritual. *Exousia* is the authority mentioned in Acts 8:19, when Simon saw that the Holy Spirit was imparted by the laying on of hands: "'Give this authority to me as well, so that everyone on whom I lay my hands may receive the Holy Spirit" (NASB).

But the authority I'd like to focus on is a royal authority that comes through the laying-on of hands. It's the Hebrew word *semikhah*—also transliterated as *smicha*. It means both authority and also the ceremony of laying on of hands to pass on that authority. (Christians didn't invent the laying on of hands; that already existed in the Old Testament.)

Here's an example. Moses led two or three million people through the desert. He wasn't overly excited to be a leader in the first place, so he was probably relieved to pass on duties to Joshua. When the time came to pass on leadership, Moses didn't just tell everyone, "OK. Here's your new leader." Moses laid hands on Joshua. This process wasn't just a ceremony for show; it was an act of the transference of real authority. It was and is a powerful act.

That's why Scripture tells us not to lay hands on someone prematurely. If you give authority to a basket case, they're going to be a basket case with all your authority. The scriptural caution doesn't mean "Be super cautious about putting people in a leadership position." It means: "Be careful who you're giving your authority to."

I was a police officer for a number of years during a very chaotic time in Belfast. People were being killed right and left. People would come to police officers' houses and put bombs under our cars. We had to check our cars every morning to make sure they weren't booby-trapped.

Picture this: I'm eighteen years old, barely shaving—still got a little bit of acne—and I'm standing in uniform on a road in Northern Ireland. My instructions are to stop a vehicle that's coming toward me at thirty or forty miles an hour, filled with people who want to kill me and may be armed. I put my hand up for the vehicle to stop. The vehicle stops. Why? I have no authority in and of myself. I'm an eighteen-year-old boy who barely shaves. The car stops because they recognize the authority I'm walking in.

You only have the authority that you're submitted to.

I didn't just wake up one morning, go out and buy a police uniform, put it on, and stand out in the middle of a road. I had to go through a whole process. I had to be trained— months and months of training. It was like a military boot camp that lasted for twenty-one weeks. It was brutal, but it was because I submitted to that process that I could put on a uniform and stand in the middle of the road, staring down people who wanted to kill me. That's authority.

The Catholic and Anglican churches practice something called apostolic succession. They believe that they can trace back—on paper—every ordained priest who has had hands laid on them by a bishop, and that bishop can trace back every laying on of hands back to Peter. It's not surprising that churches like that can withstand storms most churches cannot. That long line of authority is the *semikhah*.

Here's a version of that from Jesus' time. Every boy was trained as a rabbi (apologies to the girls). By the time a boy was six, he had to memorize the book of Leviticus, but he had to memorize it from his father's memory—nothing was written down. So, if your father didn't memorize the text well, the chances of you being a rabbi were zero. The process relied on your ancestry. If you did get to graduate, you would go into elementary school, which was called Bet Sefer

– (which means the school of the book) in this school you had to memorize the whole Torah and this would have been ages 6-12yrs old.

(An interesting note here: rabbis looked for a student who could "do greater works than they could do". That was their mandate. Sounds familiar, right?)

Then he would take an exam; the elders in his community and synagogue would test him—based not on his ability to answer questions, but on his ability to ask good questions about God and to keep the conversation about God going. The greatness of Rabbi's was to open up the conversation and keep it open. That is why, when we read of Jesus in the Temple in Luke Chapter 2, it says they were amazed at His questions; He was being tested.

If you passed this test, you would go onto the next school called The Bet Talmid (which meant the school of the disciple) this would last for 18yrs. If you didn't pass the test, you would go back to your family and work at your family's trade.

In Jesus's time, boys would also learn their father's trade. It was all about family learning. Jesus learned to be a carpenter while still going to school, but he would undergo various tests in his Rabbi training until age thirty. When a man reached thirty and had passed all the tests along the way, he was then commissioned with *semikhah*. The *semikhah* ceremony required two witnesses to release the man with authority.

When people apply to our School of Emerging Apostles, I ask for two witnesses. I ask for a pastoral recommendation, and I ask for a spiritual father or mother. And if they're the same person, then I'll ask you to find another witness for me. Two witnesses: I want someone with authority.

Jesus's two witnesses were John the Baptist, "Behold, the Lamb of God who takes away the sin of the world!" (John 1:29 NASB) and the voice of the Father, "This is my beloved Son, in whom I am well pleased" (Matthew 3:17 NASB). When a rabbi laid hands on his next spiritual son in the process of *semikhah*, he would use words similar to "He judges, he judges. He knows, he knows." Under the New Covenant, the language of the transference of authority become more relational. The Father passed on His authority to a son, not a servant. I would suggest that this is THE model for the transference of authority, it is given to sons and daughters, not simply students. When I lay hands on people, I use the declaration: "this is my beloved daughter (or son), in whom I am well pleased."

Those were the words of transference of authority. That's not immediately obvious when reading the Scripture. We tend to think, "Oh, the Father was really proud of Jesus." No: those words indicate the transference of authority from Heaven to Jesus. That's *exousia*. When Scripture talks about Jesus teaching as one with authority, that's what it means. He's teaching as a rabbi with the authority of everything that came before Him.

This transference of authority was and is powerful. I hope you see that I'm not talking about laying hands on people and saying, "I'm just commissioning you to be amazing. Go be amazing! There's nothing the Father can't do, and he commissioned Jesus. There's nothing Jesus can't do, and He has commissioned us and tells us we will do greater works. We are supposed to be doing greater works than the One for whom nothing is impossible.

Some people have a visceral reaction to authority because we have all had bad experiences with authority. Maybe we were stopped by that cop who was just nasty. Maybe we had abusive fathers or even mothers. And we've probably all had that one pastor…

Kris Vallotton from Bethel Church in Redding, California says that when you react in error, you will produce error. So, when you react in error to a bad case of authority in your life, the result will probably be error. Why is there so much authority-related error in the Church? Maybe because, instead of granting people authority through the process of *se-*

*mikhah*, we've just said, "Go be awesome! I'll be here if you need anything." That is not empowering. In fact, it is a reaction to fear of control; it's a case of someone having experienced controlling, bad authority and not dealing with it or reacting to it in a healthy way.

It is not controlling to empower people.

When I was a young man living away from home, my mom used to call me and say, "Hey, does your phone make outgoing calls?" I just assumed: Mom's always there. I don't need to connect. When I was seventeen, I told her, "I'm going away. Heard this rumor there's a bus that leaves London, and we're going to try and find it." Buses used to leave the UK and go all over Europe. My friends and I had heard of one that was going to the South of France. The fare cost something like five pounds—it was 1982. So, in an era before cell phones, I told my mom, "We're going away. We'll be gone for about two weeks. If it's longer, don't worry about me."

Five weeks later, I called her. Collect. "Hey. Mom, just made it back to London. I have no money." Do you think the heart of my mother while I was away was, "Oh, I released him to go. If he needs me, he'll call me." That's not family, my mom was worried about me and longed to connect with me. She loved me and cared for me, even though I hadn't yet learned how important love and care were; I hadn't learned the power of healthy connection.

Authority is always in the context of connection. I don't want to be out there on my own, walking around the planet, saying, "I'm an apostle. No one can touch me." I want family. I want brothers and sisters, I want sons and daughters, I want people to be with me for this journey.

Authority also has boundaries. If I walk into your house and tell you how to decorate, how to spend your money, how to treat your children, I have overstepped the limitations of my authority. I have zero authority in your home and taking authority where I have no responsibility is abusive.

# 3: CONNECTION & PROVISION

I have encountered so many apostles who have not been empowered to do their work. They were sent out by networks that boast that they don't control people, but really, they are not empowering people. These floundering apostles crave connection. And they need it.

I'm part of the Bethel Leaders Network, as are hundreds of people all throughout the world. This connects me with a group of people that I love and am committed to. Relationships that have been built for years have resulted in some people pulling on me from within this network. It is not hierarchical, it is relational, people recognizing the grace that is on my life and drawing from that grace. I do the same with others from that network. For those who draw on me, I position myself as not responsible *for* them, but I do have responsibilities *toward* them if we want to see them succeed. And you don't see people succeed by saying, "Go, be awesome. Be as individual as you can."

God is preparing us for something that has not been seen on the earth before. To be ready, we need unity. And you know how you get unity? The five-fold. You don't get unity by destroying the five-fold and making us all equal orphans.

A disconnected orphan spirit is very familiar with a poverty spirit. I am convinced that God is going after the spirit of poverty. I've had so many conversations with people who tell me they have no money. I keep hearing, "I don't have enough. I don't know if there's going to be enough." I think that needs to be broken off of our lives.

Say you spend fifteen hours flying on a super-saver flight that would normally be three hours long—just to save $200. You can never get those fifteen hours back, but you can get the $200 bucks back. I'm not saying you should upgrade to first class but stewarding your resources well doesn't necessarily mean pinching pennies. Have you heard the rumor that He owns the cattle on a thousand hills? When we truly believe in our good Father and His promises, it changes how we think—how we live.

Picture the image of the New Jerusalem—which I believe is the Church—whose streets are paved with gold. Now picture a church that doesn't have enough money to pay the bills. There is a disconnect there, and I think God is out to fix that.

How? By raising up apostles. So, let's look at this aspect of apostles before getting back to authority.

# LACKING NOTHING

Have you heard the story that apostles were emissaries from Rome sent to establish and maintain Roman culture in the cities they conquered? After extensive research, I can find nothing to support that. It may be true, but I can find no firm, credible, evidence of it. If such evidence exists, I would love to know about it. It does appear though that they did act as emissaries for the one who sent them, people with the authority to act as the voice and hand of the one who sent them.

The Greek word *apostolos* seems to have been used for an admiral of sorts and also for the ships he would have taken and the men he would have led. Originally used as an adjective with an emphasis on being sent, it then became a word used for the fleet itself, the entire naval expedition. I would advocate for "Fleet" being used as the collective noun for a group of apostles. Let's see if it catches on.

There is also the story that Jesus gave a secular title to the apostles so that people would understand the apostles' role was to reach the world and bring a certain culture with them.

In fact, what I have found is the complete opposite. There seems to be a clear relationship between the Hebrew *sheliaH* (*shallah*) and the Greek word *Apostolos*. A *shallah* was an emissary endowed with the legal right to act as the voice and hand of the one who sent him. Just like the apostle. Apostles were also members of the Sanhedrin. They had one job apart from governing, and that one job was to collect money. Their job was to collect the Temple tax. They were sent out in twos to do this, and they weren't allowed to bring anything with them. And the synagogues where they collected this temple tax were supposed to look after them. Sound familiar?

Jesus sent his apostles out in twos, told them not to bring anything with them, and that the people they went to were supposed to look after them. Jesus then asked them, "Did you lack for anything?"

Here's a game-changer: the mark of an apostolic culture is that there is no lack for anything.

If that's the case, then one of the marks of an apostle is that you'll lack for nothing. Especially because you're going to have to transfer that "lack of lack"—that abundance—to the people who follow you. In my opinion, part of the apostolic anointing is that the people following you should be lacking for nothing. Talk about changing our thinking!

I'd like to include a side note here. In Jesus's time, only people over age twenty paid Temple tax. How many disciples had to pay? One: Peter. Only Peter and Jesus paid the Temple tax; the rest of the disciples were under twenty. In fact, John may have been about fifteen or sixteen. Imagine raising up apostles who are fifteen and sixteen years old and saying, "All authority is given unto you. Now go." I once heard someone say, "If anybody appears and thinks they're an apostle, and they're under forty years old, ignore them. They're a false apostle." Considering the fact that Jesus was crucified in His early thirties, that doesn't really make sense. All that to say; this is another reminder to examine our assumptions of what an apostle can look like.

So back to apostles bringing financial freedom wherever they go. The first-century historian Josephus tells us that in Jesus's time, it took ten thousand soldiers to bring in all the gold that was collected from taxes. That's a problem I'd like to have. That's a problem I think every church in this country would like to have: needing ten thousand soldiers to bring in all the money.

Lacking nothing is possible with the right authority and alignment.

## FOLLOW ME

Remember that rabbis were looking for students who could do greater works that they could. They would approach a child and say: "follow me." And then the rabbi would walk away. Every Hebrew boy was longing for the day when someone would come up to him and say, "follow me." They dreamed about it. It was like getting picked for the NFL.

Imagine the conversation: "What would you do, John?" "I don't know Andrew, what would you do?" "I think I'd like to abandon everything—my nets, everything. I don't think I'd even tell my family. I wouldn't even look back. I'd just go." They dreamed about the day when someone would come and say, "follow me." Sound familiar?

Jesus tells a couple of the disciples-to-be, "Follow me. I will make you fishers of men." Some context: Jesus wasn't a poor worker eking a living out of making furniture for IKEA. He was the Tony Robbins of His time. People would take three days off work to come and listen to His wisdom because He was a rabbi with authority. Crowds of 5000 and 7000 people gathered around him and stayed, even without food. We would call that revival. It was Jesus walking in authority.

After one of those meetings, Jesus makes that famous request: "Follow me, and I will make you fishers of men." He didn't say, "Take my business card" or "Here's my vision statement." He said, "follow me."

It's so simple, but we've made it so complicated. And I'd like to point out that the people he asked to follow Him were not perfect. People are people. Guess what? You can be an apostle with flaws. You can be a prophet with flaws—or an evangelist, pastor, teacher. The statement that "You aren't an apostle/prophet/pastor/teacher/evangelist if you..." (fill in the blank) is simply not true. Our goal is healthy five-fold grace carriers but that requires a culture where growth is present, failures are addressed, and grace is at work, not some false standard of self-righteousness marked by words like "should" and phrases like "I would never...'

## MINISTRY IS MORE THAN A PASTOR

We must get rid of the impossible standard of perfection we have for people in ministry, and we must lift the burden/mindset that ministry = pastors. Pastors are only one of the five-fold, and yet we've dumped everything on them.

The resulting statistics are sobering:

- 1800 pastors leave the ministry every month
- 40% of pastors will not be in the ministry in ten years
- Only 10% will finish their working life as pastors
- 80% of pastors who lead a local church say that pastoring negatively affects their family life

- Almost half of pastors say they've experienced depression or burnout to the extent that they've had to take sick leave
- 72% of pastors report they work between 55-75 hours a week
- 84% of pastors feel they are on call 24/7

And the numbers of PKs (pastors' kids) not attending church because of the negative effects they've seen the church have on their family? Astronomical.

The model is broken. To fix it, we need to raise up the five-fold. We need family leadership. When people meet me, they quickly learn that I'm not pastoral in a way they are used to. If they want me to "counsel" them, I ask them three questions first:

1. Do you tithe? No? Fix that, and then come back and talk to me. Yes? Ok…
2. Are you a son or a daughter? If so, whose son or daughter, are you? "Well, I have many fathers…" Nope. Fix that.
3. Do you have any bitterness or unforgiveness in your heart? Guess what? If so, fix that…and then come and talk to me.

And if they have good answers for all three questions, their next step will be to meet with someone from a pastoral care team, not me. It's not that I don't care in fact I care about people a lot, I care that they are free, joyful, and walking in victory; it's just that I don't have the grace on my life to help you as a pastor does. I care enough to say, "let me show you someone who can help".

So many church leaders who are called pastors aren't really five-fold pastors. That has confused things. The church leader may not even have any five-fold gift, they are simply leading and are the overseer for the congregation. When we say of someone, "They're very pastoral," we often mean that they are filled with mercy. Real pastors, the shepherds among us, look after the sheep, they protect us from wolves and lions. The model of the shepherd is the Lord who according to Psalms 23 means that under a shepherd's watch, we lack nothing. The shepherd—the pastor—has an anointing to provide. Removing lack is a pastoral anointing.

But there is a problem with that. Almost two-thirds of church leaders say they don't get a livable wage. We have installed "pastors" in churches who have a spirit of poverty and lack all over them and under the guise of the "humble pastor" we have accepted a spirit of lack and poverty rather than of provision and wanting for nothing. Once again, we need to readjust our thinking.

# 4: THE FIVE-FOLD & UNITY

I've taken my time getting to the five-fold itself because it was important to emphasize the need to change our thinking, to understand authority, and to be connected and lacking nothing. That's our starting point. Now, we're ready to move forward.

> "Therefore I, the prisoner of the Lord, implore you to walk in a manner worthy of the calling with which you have been called..." (Ephesians 4:1 NASB).

We are supposed to be walking in a manner worthy of our calling. If the gospel is a sin-management program, we will read this to mean: "stay sin free." This has nothing to do with sex, drugs, and Rock 'n' Roll. Neither does this have to do with wearing a shirt and tie and donning the façade of righteousness. Yet that's how the Church has interpreted this verse.

Paul is writing the Ephesians to set the stage for them to be powerful. To walk in a manner worthy of your calling means walking in a manner worthy of someone who calls themselves a child of the Most High God: one who walks in authority. Walk in that manner—not the manner of someone who pretends not to drink a beer. Do you ever have those meals where you're out with Christians, and everyone waits to see who orders first? "I'll have a non-alcoholic beer please." Or, "I'll just take a water." Truthfully, I'm the guy who'll say, "I'll have a Manhattan, please." Because walking in a manner worthy of our calling is not sin-management.

Paul is describing what it looks like when the five-fold is in operation; we should all feel more powerful when you're around the five-fold, more hopeful, more courageous—not less.

Remember when Jesus's disciples start to argue about who was the greatest? Notice that Jesus doesn't correct them. In fact, He tells them: No, those seats are already taken. And even when they get their mum in on the act, He doesn't correct them for walking in a manner worthy of their calling.

When you're around the healthy five-fold, you start to get the sense that anything is possible. That maybe you *can* do things through Christ who strengthens you. That maybe there's hope things won't be like they are forever. The reason for this sense of possibility? You are going to walk in the authority of your Rabbi, Jesus.

> Therefore I, the prisoner of the Lord, implore you to walk in a manner worthy of the calling with which you have been called, with all humility and gentleness, with patience, showing tolerance for one another in love, being diligent to preserve the unity of the Spirit in the bond of peace. (Ephesians 4:1-3 NASB)

The five-fold will bring unity: unity of the Spirit, not of agreement, not of doctrine, not of dogma. When someone stands up and teaches the rapture, I'm not going to declare, "I can no longer fellowship with you, because I don't believe in the rapture." No! It's about the unity of the spirit. What if we responded to difference like this: "Oh, you believe that? OK. Great. Let's go see some miracles happen together. Let's go shift the atmosphere somewhere." And do you know how important the rapture becomes at that moment? Of zero importance. Because we're working together in the unity of the Spirit in the bond of peace. It's not the unity of agreement.

Jonathan Welton and I agree on some things and disagree on others, but we have the unity of the Spirit. When he visited our School of Emerging Apostles, some of the most fun times were when he would ask, "What do you think about this?" And I'm like, "I don't agree with you. I think it's this…." And Jonathan would say, "Oh, fascinating." I love that about Jonathan and other great leaders, the ability to hold a differing position and not lose relationship. After all, I assume that I will continue to grow, to learn, to be adjusted. That means I may not believe everything I now believe in ten years' time.

Let's learn to do that. Let's learn to be fascinated. When it comes to nonessentials, instead of saying, "how wrong!" how about saying, "how fascinating!" Let's preserve the unity of the Spirit in the bond of peace. Can we do that? And if that's not a big enough challenge, how about we still walk together if we disagree about moral issues? But that's a challenge for another day….

The church I attend is pretty diverse. We even have Republicans and Democrats breaking bread together. Talk about miracles, right? Politics will not change a thing. Let's stop fighting and start cultivating unity of the Spirit with the bond of peace.

> [There is] one body and one Spirit, just as also you were called in one hope of your calling; one Lord, one faith, one baptism, one God and Father of all who is over all and through all and in all. But to each one of

us grace was given according to the measure of Christ's gift. Therefore, it says, "WHEN HE ASCENDED ON HIGH, HE LED CAPTIVE A HOST OF CAPTIVES, AND HE GAVE GIFTS TO MEN." (Ephesians 4:4-8 NASB)

He's not being gender-specific here. These gifts are for all of mankind, for humanity.

(Now this *expression*, "He ascended," what does it mean except that He also had descended into the lower parts of the earth? He who descended is Himself also He who ascended far above all the heavens, so that He might fill all things.) **And He gave some [as] apostles, and some [as] prophets, and some [as] evangelists, and some [as] pastors and teachers, for the equipping of the saints for the work of service, to the building up of the body of Christ; until we all attain to the unity of the faith, and of the knowledge of the Son of God, to a mature man, to the measure of the stature which belongs to the fullness of Christ.** As a result, we are no longer to be children, tossed here and there by waves and carried about by every wind of doctrine, by the trickery of men, by crafti-

> ness in deceitful scheming…. (Ephesians 4:
> 9-14 NASB, emphasis mine)

Sometimes, these gifts are called The Ascension gifts. Other times they are called the gifts of Jesus. Whatever we call them, the bolded section of this Scripture is a source text for the five-fold, comprising apostles, prophets, evangelists, pastors, teachers. And here is another source text:

> And God has appointed in the church, first
> apostles, second prophets, third teachers,
> then miracles, then gifts of healings, helps,
> administrations, [various] kinds of tongues
> (I Corinthians 12:28 NASB).

This is where we encounter one of our major misunderstandings about the apostles; since they are listed first, they have been considered Number One. I want to debunk that completely.

This is how the Corinthians verse should be translated: "First of all, apostles." It's chronology, not hierarchy. Who did Jesus raise up first? Apostles. Why?

> …it is much truer that the members of the
> body which seem to be weaker are neces-
> sary; and those members of the body which

> we deem less honorable, on these we bestow
> more abundant honor... (1 Corinthians
> 12:22-23 NASB)

Apostles are described in 1 Corinthians 4:10-11 as being the "dishonored" members. In the context of a human body, apostles are the reproductive organs of the Body. They are the unseemly parts. The bits you would cover with your bikini. Seriously: Paul is referring to the physical reproductive organs that we cover up. *That's* what apostles are. We're reproductive. We reproduce. Apostles were appointed by Jesus first simply because the grace itself allows apostles to raise up, empower, and deploy all of the other five-fold graces.

I am connected with many churches, and some of them have labeled an apostle's seat on the stage. If we think of the apostle as Numero Uno, that maybe makes sense. But it's *not* about apostles being Numero Uno. We must get away from the connection between "apostle" as status and beginning recognizing "apostle" as a task.

Jesus made apostles "first of all" because apostles are the only ones who can reproduce the other five-fold. Then the prophets start to appear. In the New Covenant, there would have been no prophets, pastors, teachers, or evangelists without there first being apostles, but that doesn't mean the apostle is in charge—it's not a ruling function. In the New Testament, the elders do the ruling. So first come the apostles, then the prophets, then the evangelists, then the pastors, then the teachers. Each five-fold grace will reproduce according to kind, except for the apostle whose grace allows him or her to reproduce all of the five-fold.

Connecting the "unseemly" parts of the body in 1 Corinthians 12 to the apostle, Jonathan Welton also talks about the excretory gift of the apostle. In other words, part of an apostle's role is to eliminate the crap. Yes, I said that. It's part of an apostle's job to say, "This is toxic. It's time for it to go."

And one of the toxic thoughts to eliminate is that apostles are the most important of the five-fold. Our current models of apostles are the Randy Clarks, the Bill Johnsons, the Che Ahns the Heidi Bakers, etc. All of these men and women have contributed absolutely amazing things to the Body of Christ over decades. They have altered the course of the church and impacted nations. They have enormous followings and while being personally humble, they have been promoted by God. If these are our main source for understanding what an apostle looks like, we will associate being an apostle with fame and status. If you feel called with the grace of an apostle but you measure yourself up against Randy Clark, you're going to walk around thinking either you have to be like Randy Clark or you're not an apostle. We have to change our thinking.

Let's look at some distinctions for each of the five-fold.

**Apostles**

If you're following an apostle, you'll be like the apostle. Paraphrasing Acts 2:42: those following the apostles continued steadfastly in the apostles' doctrine. If you're following an apostle, you will be like the apostle. That's what apostolic means; it means apostle-like. Of course, you'll have your own personality and expression—and we'll talk about that later—but you can't be apostolic without following an apostle. Believing you can be apostolic because you listen to a church's podcast long-distance is nonsense. Where's the family in that? Family is about relationship. An apostle is not your apostle if he or she doesn't know who you are. That's why we need more apostles.

If someone's an apostle which means they have the ability to reproduce apostles and the other five-fold, they are invited to bring alignment and correction to churches and bring Heaven to earth. If that apostle also has the gift of leadership, they will most likely be successful and visible with influence beyond average. They are leaders who are also an apostle. But you don't have to be a leader to be an apostle. We have to be careful not to confuse Romans 12 with Ephesians 4. Romans 12 describes the gift of leadership. Ephesians 4 describes the graces of the five-fold. One of the biggest mistakes I see in understanding the grace of an apostle is the confusion with the gift of leadership.

**Prophets**

My wife, Rachel, is a prophet and teaches the prophetic. She teaches three different expressions of prophecy:

1. There is the ability to prophesy—and anyone can prophesy
2. There is the gift of prophecy
3. There is what some call the office of the prophet (though I prefer calling it the grace of the prophet)

We tend to get these confused. Prophets don't necessarily have the biggest gift of prophecy; that's someone with a really good gift of prophecy. And a leader can operate with a really good gift of prophecy, but that doesn't make him or her a prophet. I would actually argue that if the person who is called a prophet is the most anointed in the gift of prophecy in their realm of influence, they actually are either not a prophet, or don't understand what a prophet does. The prophet's job, like the rest of the five-fold, is to equip people to do greater works than we can do.

I'd also like to caution against reducing the gift of prophecy by thinking someone operating in it must be a prophet—or must be "promoted" to a prophet. That's like saying that the gift of prophecy is not good enough.

So, what does a prophet do? Prophets raise up other prophets. A healthy prophet does not need to be the most prophetic person in their sphere. They want, in fact, I would say they *need* to raise up other people. Prophets bring correction and alignment to churches. Prophecy doesn't correct but prophets do.

My wife is surrounded by prophets she has raised up, and if she goes somewhere to prophesy, she wants to bring her team to come with her, because they're even better than she is. Prophets see the potential in people and call it out.

Rachel and I recently met with a couple, and my wife said of the woman: "You are a prophet. I can see it all over you." The woman said, "I don't even prophesy!" Rachel responded, "Well, let's fix that." It is the honor of a prophet to raise up a prophetic company; that's what prophets do. They equip, equip, equip.

Along with the apostle, prophets change the culture of churches and regions.

**Evangelists**

We tend to think that the person who goes everywhere evangelizing is an evangelist. Why do we think that? I think it is because we want everybody to be five-fold, we seem to see it is the pinnacle of Christian ministry. Meanwhile, we're not being equipped, we submit to no authority, and we don't know what we're doing because we're looking for a bumper sticker or car magnet that says, "Five-Fold Evangelist."

If you are an evangelist, I want to know: are you equipping people to share their faith and to clean the fish? Because being fishers of men means not just catching the fish, but cleaning the fish, too. When you look at Church history, evangelists aren't just the ones out there preaching, they're also the ones helping clean you up and getting you healthy and ready for the pastor.

**Pastors**

One of the major false assumptions we make about pastors is that they are a five-fold pastor because they're really caring or merciful.

Danny Silk is a five-fold pastor. I know him a bit, and he has the authority to speak into my life, to adjust me, to correct me. But he's not what you'd think of as merciful. Danny is ruthless—in a good way. He'll point at me and say, "This needs to be fixed. Whatever's going on, you need to fix it. Do you know what's going on?"

Someone once told me, "Sheep are dumb. They'll go wherever the food is. Make sure you're feeding your people, so they won't scatter." That's not what sheep do. Sheep don't follow food. Sheep follow a shepherd. If you go to Ireland and you see a field dotted with sheep, you'll notice that the minute the shepherd calls for them, they'll all come running. They'll leave their food to run after the shepherd because they know the shepherd always has something better. Sheep don't follow food, they follow a shepherd. And sheep don't like to drink from rushing water; that's why shepherds—pastors—lead you beside still waters.

Five-fold pastors will lead you to still waters. You know you're around a five-fold pastor because you feel safe in the middle of rough waters. Psalm 23 is a model of shepherding. The shepherd reminds us: "Even though the enemy tried to take you down, he didn't succeed. In fact, why don't we tell that story of triumph in front of the enemy? I'm going to set a table here in the presence of your enemies, and I'm going to declare: 'You weren't able to take me down.'" This is what five-fold pastors look like. And goodness and mercy will then follow you all the days of your life. The Hebrew word for goodness, *towb*, can be translated as wealth. Imagine wealth following you all the days of your life!

Five-fold pastors hold the head of a giant that they've just cut off with a sword and say, "This is all for Jesus." We call King

David, who penned Psalms 23, the shepherd-king. That's a beautiful description of a five-fold pastor. And because of that gift, we lack for nothing.

## Teachers

Teachers have a passion for truth, but five-fold teachers also equip us. They don't just tell us what to believe, but they equip us to study, to research, to understand the Bible, and to see Heaven come. If we're not seeing a breakthrough in healing, teachers will take us deep into what Scripture says and help us to see what God has already spoken to us about healing.

As with all of the five-fold, alignment is really important. A five-fold teacher who is aligned with an apostle will teach what is important to the apostle. Dann Farrelly is Bethel Church's in-house, five-fold teacher, and he is a great example of this. He is a phenomenal teacher who helps people learn what it looks like to bring Heaven to earth—which is the heart of the apostle of his church.

That's the job of the five-fold teacher: to align to their apostle's heart and equip people to understand and live the truth of that vision.

It should not be confused with the Romans 12 gift of teaching or the church elder's ability to be "apt to teach." All those who teach are not five-fold teachers.

# 5: CORRECTING MISCONCEPTIONS

Here are a few more helpful clarifications for understanding the five-fold.

## NOBODY'S PERFECT

I mentioned earlier that apostles aren't perfect. No one is perfect. In fact, one of the apostles—Judas—killed himself. We think, "Well, he couldn't possibly be an apostle, could he?" Yet Jesus called him one. Are we being so afraid of raising up a Judas that we stop raising up eleven apostles?

Peter: what a loudmouth, right? There are contemporary Peters who are called to be apostles, but because they're a little bit erratic and they speak before they think, we write them off: they couldn't possibly be apostles, right?

What about Timothy? He's very nervous, a couple of women in his church nag him, and he needs to get on the wine at night just to ease his nerves. Timothy? Wimpy! Couldn't be an apostle.

Or Junias. She couldn't be an apostle because—she's a woman! (An aside: there were more apostles mentioned in Scripture apart from the original twelve.)

And then there's Paul. He was the scariest dude on the planet. He goes from being a feared persecutor of Christians who has an encounter with Jesus that changed everything, to be a teacher of Christians. He couldn't endure any sort of *laissez-faire* laid-back-ness; he was entering churches and scaring people with his harsh delivery of the truth. Can you imagine the most hated religious or political leader you know, who has opposed the Church for years, entering your church foyer and saying, "I got saved, I'm born again. Hallelujah! I'd like to teach." Paul? Scary! Couldn't be an apostle.

People aren't perfect.

After Judas kills himself, the apostles need a replacement. Keep in mind Jesus's selection process for the apostles: he prayed all night. He didn't do a six-month search process. He prayed. Then He just said, "Hey, I want you twelve to be my apostles.

Interestingly, instead of asking the Holy Spirit for help in choosing Judas's replacement, the apostles revert to an old-covenant method. They roll the die and select two people: Matthias and Justus. Matthias gets the gig. But then he's never heard from again. Ever.

Justus didn't get picked. But he is mentioned again in Acts 15 in Paul and Silas's close company. He's Paul's buddy. In fact, Justus—the guy who was *not* picked to be an apostle—is the one in Acts 15 told to deliver the verdict from the council in Jerusalem. What does this tell us? It is just as important what you do with *not* getting chosen as it is getting chosen. It's just as important how you deal with disappointment as it is with success. In fact, it may be more important.

## THE CHURCH DOESN'T HURT PEOPLE—PEOPLE HURT PEOPLE

Since we are all flawed, the five-fold does not operate perfectly. Sometimes we get hurt or we hurt others. To say, "I have been hurt by the Church" isn't true. We get hurt by people. I've been hurt by my children, but that doesn't stop me wanting to stay in relationship with my children—to keep loving them even through heartache or pain. The Church doesn't hurt people. People hurt people.

When my wife and I were in Ireland recently, we had the privilege of praying for one of the elders named Alistair from our old church there. It was a church of about 1200 people.

We had arrived there in 1994 hurt by our experiences at the church I had been saved and discipled in. Stuff that I'd done and hadn't handled well, and stuff that people in the church had done and hadn't handled well. We actually ended up leaving the church pretty well; we met with the elders, we blessed them, we asked them to lay hands on us and release us and we remain real friends with those elders to this day.

So, we had started attending this church where Alistair was an elder. He came and met my wife and me in our house one night and said, "I'm here to talk about membership. I think you should join the church."

I said, "Only Jesus decides who's a member of a church and really, what is the church anyway?" (The typical response of a hurt person) I told him, "I can't do it. We have been so hurt."

He said, "OK. I need you to give me permission to hurt you again."

"Whaaaaat? What are you talking about?"

But truly, it makes total sense. People hurt people. But we need to *restore* the standard, not keep the sub-standard. When the standard has been knocked down through our interactions and relationships, our job is not to maintain and advocate for an inferior standard. Our job—in forgiveness—

is to restore the standard as if it never happened. So, yes, we have to give others permission to hurt us again. It will probably be unintentional, but we're just people doing the best we can. And the hurt we carry can stop us from receiving the grace others carry on our lives.

## NOT EVERYBODY IS FIVE-FOLD

I'll repeat that: Not everybody is five-fold. As it says in Ephesians 4: *some* apostles, *some* prophets, *some* evangelists, *some* pastors, *some* teachers. And this doesn't mean you just distribute everyone in the Church into one of the five-fold roles. That's not what Paul is saying. God has actually set apart *some* people to carry this grace on their life. And the reason? Look at Ephesians 4:12-13: "…for the equipping of the saints for the work of service to the building up of the body of Christ; until we all attain to the unity of faith…" (NASB).

A quick side note: if anyone questions whether the five-fold are still in operation, the "until" there is my proof text that they are still in existence: "…until we attain…" which later ends with "…the fullness of Christ." I don't think we've reached that unity and fullness. Therefore, what we call the five-fold gifts are still in operation.

Back to not everyone being five-fold. Over the last twenty years or so, many in the Church have been focused on leadership. There are leadership summits, we're raising up leaders, everybody's a leader, anybody can be a leader! What we've done is communism—or socialism, if that term is easier for you. We've made everybody the same, and we've made every definition of leader the same.

My old church used to have leadership meetings, but we were never sure where to draw the line of who was a leader and who wasn't a leader. So, the guy who did the overhead projectors—remember overhead projectors? —he would come to our leader meetings. I remember asking, "What is he leading? He's not leading, he's serving." I didn't mean it as a negative; I just didn't want to see the role of service reduced. If we think leadership is the top of some hierarchy, then we're saying service is less important.

We do this with the five-fold all the time. We see a person with a gift of mercy, but we don't think that mercy is so important, so we call him or her a five-fold pastor. We see a gifted prophetic person but somehow the Holy Spirit's gift is not good enough, so we need to call them a Prophet. We see a gifted Romans 1 leader but again, that is not good enough, God's gift does not meet our ego standards, so we say they are an apostle.

Let's not dilute one gift by wanting the title of another.

# KEEP THE MAIN THING
# THE MAIN THING

At the end of the day, we have to remember it's all about the Kingdom and the King. It's all about getting that beautiful truth out into the world.

I was baptized in the Holy Spirit in 1987. I was still a police officer at that time, so I was walking around in uniform, looking all macho, ready to take on the world…but I couldn't stop crying! I would say to my buddy, "God is so good! He's just so good!" This friend of mine was hardcore.

He called me about a year after I moved to the US and told me this story.

> I thought I'd share this with you. I was in my garden, and I heard, "I'm comin' for you." An audible voice: "I'm comin' for you." I thought my time was up. I thought they were coming to get me. I thought the Provisional IRA were coming to take me out in my own home. So, I went down and took cover. I drew my firearm, crept into the garage, and got my long-arm, and I heard it again, "I'm comin' for you." And it wasn't the voice of a terrorist, it was the voice of

> God. I remembered you telling me He was
> so good…. I gave my life to Jesus right there
> on the spot. And I felt all this darkness leave
> my body.

This guy got saved and delivered because he'd heard that God was so good.

He *is* ridiculously good. *That's* what we're supposed to be telling people.

We should be going around saying, "Let me tell you what God did in my life…." "I was lost and now I'm found." "Let me tell you how good He is." That doesn't make you an evangelist. That makes you a Christian. You *should* have the Holy Spirit drop on you and be able to prophesy at a heartbeat. You're a Christian. We *should* care for people. Not because we're pastoral, because we're Christians.

# 6: WHAT'S YOUR PALETTE?

Let's talk about dippings. I am borrowing this idea from my friend, Jonathan Welton, who created a really useful illustration for the five-fold. Picture five, big barrels, each filled with a different color of paint.

Say the prophet barrel is full of yellow paint. At some point, say you get dipped in the grace of being a prophet; you start forthtelling things, you're growing and learning, you're equipping the body, you're changing the culture around you into a prophetic culture. This grace just seems to be on your life. You've been dipped in that grace—yellow. And everybody knows you're a prophet because it's visible—you're yellow. You walk around and people say, "She's totally a prophet. She commands something that's not as if it were. She's always calling out the gold in people."

My wife is the most encouraging person on the planet. I love it. I love being married to someone who, when I'm not being my best self, tells me, "That's not who you are. *This* is who you are. *This* is what I see in you." She is completely encouraging. You can't *not* be encouraging when you're a new-covenant prophet. People will recognize it.

Then, other stuff starts happening; you feel like you're changing a little bit. Another grace seems to be appearing, and people start to say, "I think God is shifting you from prophet to apostle." Metaphorically, you're dipped in the apostle barrel—say it's red. If a prophet who's yellow is dipped in red, what's is the resulting apostle color? Orange. And that orange will be a different hue than another prophet-turned-apostle.

Say the evangelist barrel is filled with blue paint, and you're blue—you're an evangelist. You're going all around, catching fish and then skinning, gutting, cleaning—getting them ready to hand over to the pastor who can help them get and stay healthy.

Then you start to get prophetic words, and people start to relate to you a bit differently. They start to relate to you in a way that draws a different grace from your life. You receive a prophetic word that you're transitioning to an apostle, and guess what? You get dipped in the red of the apostle. What color are you now? Purple.

You can continue that idea with all the rest of the five-fold. No one is going to look the same. There are no exact color matches. Say you've got speckles of white discernment throughout your orange apostle-prophet palette, and your gift of faith appears as drops of green, and then a large swath of peace appears as another color. Even if you run into another prophet-turned-apostle, you are going to look completely different from each other. Everyone is their own version of a Jackson Pollock painting.

I have a dominant personality, and I'm an apostle. If I am the primary apostle someone encounters, they might think every apostle has a dominant personality. Not true. Not only do we wear different "colors" or "dippings", throw into the mix our different personalities, and the variety is endless. You don't have to look exactly like me to be an apostle. In fact: I wouldn't want you to, and you shouldn't want to: that's a clone. We're not looking for clones, but we are looking for resemblance. This is about family; we're looking for sons and daughters.

I have three kids. My two boys are strikingly handsome and my daughter's beautiful, and everyone who sees photographs of them says, "They all look like Rachel." Yes, they look like their mother, but they resemble me, too.

When people look at you, they often see a bit of your father and mother in you. But you don't look exactly like our father because your mother is in you as well. We have to break this notion that there is one type of apostle out there, and it looks like a 50- or 60-year-old white guy with a huge ministry and global influence. Unfortunately, that's often the only model we've been exposed to.

One weekend when Danny Silk spoke at our church, a young African-American girl sang, "I'm no longer a slave to fear." Danny turned around to me and said, "That song has never been sung that well before." We were being led into the Spirit realm—into the throne room of Heaven—by a seventeen-year-old black girl who probably doesn't have everything together. *That's* Kingdom. I want *those* apostles. Not just the 53-year-old white guys with cute accents.

## HONORING OUR GIFTS

It is important to honor our differences. And part of honoring those differences is by not assuming everyone is five-fold. Calling someone an evangelist when they're operating from a gift of faith is not just unhelpful, it's also disrespectful to the Holy Spirit. It's assuming that the gifts of the Holy Spirit are not enough, and therefore I'm going to go for the gifts of Jesus. If we think we have to promote people into Jesus's gifts just because they're "only" manifesting the Spirit's gift, that's pretty darn insulting. It's fully OK and fully wonderful to say, "I have the gift of faith to see God come on the streets when I'm out there telling people the good news. That's my gift.

I'm not an evangelist. Sure, I have a gift for miracles, but that doesn't mean I'm an evangelist."

It's OK to be proud of your gift. By doing so, you are honoring the gift the Holy Spirit gave you without pretending it's something else for the sake of your ego.

## LET'S GET HEALTHY

God does new things. He has a habit of doing a new thing every generation or so and by now, you would think we would be used to it.

The challenge for those with whom God did a new thing with from a previous generation is to recognize and at least not get in the way of what He is doing now.

I have frequently encountered Godly men and women getting upset as new apostles emerge. They are not bad people, maybe they fear being left behind, maybe they have values that need to be adjusted, I don't really know. I do know that God is doing a new thing, not the old thing version 2.0 and that will require all of us, to be healthy. Health is defined as not being afraid, recognizing and working on our insecurities (and yes, we all have them), allowing ourselves to be vulnerable, and not resisting what God is doing.

I'd like to suggest that the devil is not trying to populate hell. He is not, as the cartoons depict, the king of hell trying to rule as many people as possible. His destiny is a lake of fire and his fear is that the Kingdom advances here on earth. His fear is that everybody starts to do what they're called to do and diminish his influence on earth. He's terrified of it. We should not be helping him.

Let's all walk in our gifts and callings in health and unity. Let's terrify the devil.

# 7: KNOW THYSELF

Paul called himself a master architect. Apostles are architects. Based on their areas of influence, they can say to a church: this is what you should build. But apostles are not builders.

If you visit Trump Tower, you know it's Trump Tower because it says so right across it: Trump. It's a bit of a giveaway. Did Donald Trump—as he was then before he became president—did he lay one single brick in that building? No. What about the architect? Did the architect lay one single bit of rebar? No.

We don't expect the architects to be the builders, but we do expect them to be able to work things out, draw up plans, and get things started. Apostles say to a church, "Hey, you know what? I think we should emphasize this for a season, do this, cut back on this, build this." Problem is, if you make them carry out all of those plans, they'll burn out and resign. I think the statistics about pastors resigning is because they're not actually pastors. They might be prophets or apostles, but we're expecting them to be pastors, administrators, and leaders.

Apostles are architects. They plan things out. They can say: do this, do that, put this here, and you'll get some flow. And it brings up the question: is it important to call yourself an apostle if you're an apostle? It is.

I often visit a certain church. The people are just gorgeous, but they relate to me as a pastor, not an apostle. The leader of the church relates to me as an apostle, but because he has never told his congregation what to expect, they don't relate to me as an apostle. He introduces me as "My good friend, pastor Ian." I think, "Who? I'd like to meet that guy—where is he? You can't be talking about *me*. I'm not pastor Ian." His church has never been introduced to me as an apostle. So, when I go there, I risk confusing everybody. They're expecting: "Let me lead you by still waters" but instead they get: "Hey! Let's go explore the rushing river. It's amazing! The water's so much cooler and fresher, and you can kayak down it. It's fantastic." That's what they get from me.

Apostles are built for warfare. You know the expression: "I smelled blood in the water." I would say all apostles reading this are responding, "Mmmmm. I know that saying." People who are born for war think, "Let's a kick the devil in the heiny!" That is confusing if people are expecting to walk beside still waters. Instead of mellow, they get roars of "Come on! Let's take some territory. Let's go see the Kingdom come! Let's build"

It's important to identify yourself. I'm not saying to put it on your business card, but it's really helpful when people have an expectation of what they can draw on. If I have a five-fold pastor anointing, and you need to draw on that grace, great. But if I have a five-fold apostle anointing, and you try to draw pastoral anointing from me, you're going to be terribly confused. And terribly disappointed.

When people start to relate to you in one way, it can confuse the rest of your relationship with them. So, it's pretty important for me to say, "I'm not a five-fold pastor." It doesn't mean I don't care about people. I care deeply about people. Deeply. I love people—I am one! My wife and children are all people. But caring as an apostle rather than as a pastor looks different.

My wife is a prophet. But she also has the gift of mercy. My first "dipping" was as a prophet; I'm now an apostle. And we have to manage that even between ourselves. Can you imagine? Because my first dip was as a prophet and she's a prophet, we both carry big swords. And we can go after it—with each other! Honestly, sometimes we have said to each other.

"Can you put your sword away?" We need the more merciful, fatherly, and motherly side of our anointings to show up.

We need to learn how to do this. Calling people who they are is really important. Otherwise, you bring confusion. If you receive a prophet in the name of a prophet, you receive a prophet's reward. If you receive a prophet in the name of a pastor, you're going to be terribly confused. If you receive an apostle in the name of a leader, you're going to be terribly disappointed.

Personally, I get exhausted when people are pulling on the wrong thing from me. I start to ask myself, "Why am I exhausted? Oh! They're trying to pull on me as a leader. Oh, I should have switched over to that part of me because I thought I was coming in as an apostle." The worst is when people try to draw on me as a pastor. What they usually mean by that is not a five-fold shepherd but rather the mercy thing. I do have a little of the mercy gift, but it's like a thimble full. And the minute someone starts to draw on it, there it goes—it's gone! Empty. Sorry. You keep trying to draw on the mercy, but I've got nothing! I love you, but I can't give that to you. That's not the grace that's on my life. I can't give you what I don't have.

If I need a plumber, I need to know I am calling a plumber for help. If I need an electrician, I am not calling a landscaper. Sure, they may have some skills or knowledge just by being in the 'industry' and have watched others do stuff, but I want the man or woman who has a particular set of skills.

If you come to me for prayer to get fixed and sorted, I can point you in the right direction; I'll point you to the ministry team who have that grace.

Jonathan Welton describes helpful metaphors for the five-fold: apostles are the architects; prophets are the plumbers; evangelists are the electrical engineers; pastors are framers constructing the walls; and teachers put on siding, roofing, and windows.

What I like about that is the idea that we're all building something together. Who is more important: the architect or the plumber? Stupid question, right? The architect comes before the plumber does, or there's nothing to plumb, but they're both needed to build a functioning building. In fact, all five are needed to build the building. This five-fold thing is about five, strong, powerful people running together. Does there have to be an apostle in every church? Does there have to be a five-fold in every church? There doesn't *have* to be but there *can* be.

That doesn't mean we have to start a search committee for an apostle to replace the mercy driven leader we currently have. That's not the implementation of the model. It's this: if we don't have an apostle in our church, can we have one speak into our church's life? The more you expose your church to the apostle, the more you'll see the five-fold begin to pop up in your congregation—the grace just starts to spread, and apostles will emerge.

# 8: METRONS

We, however, will not boast beyond proper limits but will confine our boasting to the sphere of service God himself has assigned to us, a sphere that also includes you. We are not going too far in our boasting, as would be the case if we had not come to you, for we did get as far as you with the gospel of Christ. Neither do we go beyond our limits by boasting of work done by others. Our hope is that, as your faith continues to grow, our sphere of activity among you will greatly expand... (2 Corinthians 10:13-17 NIV).

Notice that Paul says, "We, however, will not boast beyond proper limits...." It's OK to boast! Just not beyond proper limits. I couldn't resist pointing that out.

But what I want to focus on in this passage is the word *sphere*. That is the Greek word *metron*. Our metron is our sphere of influence. Here's an example: I am not an apostle in Ireland. When I'm in Ireland, I'm just Ian. I'm not an apostle in Ireland because it's not part of my sphere/metron.

Do you know your sphere? Your metron? You can't be a five-fold without one. Otherwise, you're the apostle of your own home. You're the prophet in your own house. "Do you have a metron?' is one of the most important questions for the emerging five-fold man or woman.

I should get this right out there: I don't believe in market-place apostles, marketplace prophets, marketplace anything. You are welcome to disagree with me, but I don't believe that the marketplace is the sphere of the five-fold: The Church is. If you feel called to the political arena, great! Be a politician. If you feel called to lead in the business world, wonderful! Be a businessman or businesswoman. Those are wonderful callings. You don't need to be called an apostle to do them. You don't need to tell God: "The gift you've given me is not enough; I need to make it into something that sounds more churchy." The gift God has given you to be a business leader is amazing. The gift God has given you in the education realm doesn't mean you're a prophet. Let's not thumb our nose at God's original gift and metron. Of course, when apostles influence the church, they will inevitably influence people from other spheres and those people will look like their apostle and therefore be truly apostolic.

So, what's your metron? Say it's Indonesia. Say you have unusual favor in Indonesia that you don't have at home. We used to call you missionaries. I want to suggest that it's what you do while you're there that defines who you are. You've heard the saying, "We're human beings, not human doings." We're actually both: human beings *and* human doings. So, if you have favor in an area, what you're doing in an area will define your role.

If you think you're an apostle, and you're going to make tents in Indonesia, you're a tent maker in Indonesia until you start "apostling." Or being a prophet. Or being a pastor, or whatever. What you do defines where you're at. It is the recognition from the land and the people that affirms: "Yes, we recognize this grace on your life."

You can be a missionary and operate in any gift of the Holy Spirit. But you don't need to be five-fold. It doesn't give you upgrade status with American Airlines. It doesn't work like that.

Some missionaries are actually apostles. I am a missionary and an apostle. I left my family and everything that was important to me in Northern Ireland, and I came to America.

It's entirely possible to be an apostle in Kenya and not be an apostle in Chicago and some of that is working out who is sending you and what they are sending you to do. The definition of an apostle is someone who's sent. My wife and I didn't decide one day, "How about we just start traveling the world and see all those fine cities?" We were in conversations with our church and asked, "Will you send us? Will you lay hands on us and send us as an ambassador of this house as an apostle and prophet?"

And it's not like they laid hands on us for the sake of getting rid of us. They passed on some real authority. It's the *semikhah* stuff. When I walk into a room, I don't just walk in as myself, I walk in with the generations of histories behind me.

## SENDING

Call it licensing, commissioning, ordaining, or whatever. The process of identifying a five-fold equipper needs to be done by someone. We MUST at all costs avoid the self-appointed, self-anointed proliferation of people that have provided a start to the conversation but will not develop it further. Let me be a little clearer on that. I believe that our current conversation around the five-fold would not have happened if it was not for those forerunners who boldly stepped out and declared themselves to be apostles or prophets. They have been criticized and marginalized and I am grateful for their courage.

The time has now changed. There is now a new understanding and what worked then, will not work now. Frequently we had a poor understanding of what an apostle looked like and seldom would churches value their commissioning. Apostles were a bit like Bigfoot. Some people believed they existed, no one was ever sure if they had seen a real one, few photos existed of them, and if we are honest, the people that believed in them were a little weird. Thankfully, that is changing.

Biblically, I would suggest that the only model that exists to recognize the five-fold is the local church. Not a parachurch ministry, not a licensing organization, the local church.

I would add that there definitely seems to be Biblical precedent for Councils to exist and these seem to be made up of the leaders of local churches (elders or overseers) and apostles. It is entirely plausible for such councils to give input as I would expect from any healthy relational connection.

We teach that to affirm any gift but specifically with the five-fold, three things must be present.

1. The individual must know they are called
2. The people around them recognize this call and it is super helpful if that includes a recognized five-fold person
3. The church authority around them must recognize this call

If less than all three are present it does not mean never, it just means not yet. If only number three is not present, it does not mean that you go off and start your own ministry that now magically recognizes you are an apostle. When that happens, we limit the grace that will flow through our lives, limit the authority we will walk in, and we have effectively placed a lid on our impact and influence.

## CAN WE DO THE HARD WORK?

If you feel called to do something, but your church is not releasing you, can you figure out why? Can you work it out? That feels like a really healthy option. Here's one of the most useful things you're going to ask of your leadership: "Can you tell me how you experience me?" Most of the time we go around saying, "Let me tell you how I experience you." Totally not helpful. Truth isn't me telling you what's wrong with you. Truth is telling you what's going on inside of me and asking, "Can you tell me how you experience me?"

I have a hunch that the only people we don't release and send are the people who scare us. The people we want to tell, "I don't know what it looks like when I say "no" to you, because when I say "maybe," you sulk for three months. You withhold things, and that scares me." We don't want that person manifesting that behavior representing us.

So, ask that question: "How do you experience me?" Learn how to build favor with men and women. Be adjustable, if you believe you are called as an apostle, prophet, or whatever, have the conversation with your leaders that starts with, "What would you need from me to be released as …?"

Here are a couple of things *not* to do. Don't pull that line, "I want someone who loves me just as I am." No, no, no, no, no. Years of marriage has led me to believe that is complete nonsense. I am a different person because I have needed to be shaped, molded, and loved to be a better version of me than I was in 1989. We all need to grow.

Another thing not to do: don't say, "It's all so hard because I've been hurt." I know. That's probably the issue. Oftentimes we think hurt is healed by someone going, "There, there, there." Nope. Hurt is healed by facing the issue and being vulnerable enough to get healed. If we spend all our time protecting ourselves from ever being that vulnerable with anybody else, we are thwarting our destiny.

Where are you going? Who sent you? What are you going to do? And do you have favor there?

Find your metron. It might be a people group. It might be a gender. It might be a location. Understand that you have a metron, and without one, you can't actually be five-fold.

# 9: WALK IT OUT

How do you walk in five-fold grace? What does that look like? When you're in a church that's led by an apostle, it's common for people in that church to think they are apostles. And you might be. But just know that it's common to think you have the same grace as whatever is running through your congregation.

## RECOGNIZE THE STRUCTURE

If an administrator is leading a church, everything has to be timed perfectly; if the worship service starts thirty seconds late, you wonder if the team has been raptured…and you know there will be trouble in the staff meeting that week! If an apostle is leading a church, this is more likely the scenario: "We're starting around ten o'clock. The worship team is still praying? Fine. More glory!"

One misconception about apostles is that they're all church planters. So many apostles in the New Testament—not to mention the Early Church—never planted a church. May I remind you of poor Matthias once again. Church planters are actually…church planters.

Similar to that misconception is that apostles lead networks. Not really: administrators lead networks. If you give most apostles I know three pieces of paper to fill out, they'll never get done. In fact, for our School of Emerging Apostles, we made all the "paperwork" online. It used to be a nightmare. We made it easy; we designed it for apostles.

We held a School of the Prophets in Chicago. We wanted to build a company of prophets in Chicago who will start declaring "no gang violence." They started declaring the children of the city as children of the King. A year later, Chicago has seen a couple of hundred fewer deaths. That's Kingdom.

## RAISING UP APOSTLES

As we've seen, the five-fold is "first, apostles." It's chronology, not hierarchy. We start by raising up apostles who will run together to get the hell out of their region. Here's an example: What would it look like if poverty is destroyed in our regions? What is our model? The Kingdom. Which means there is no poor among us. According to Deuteronomy, written in a time of a lesser and weaker covenant that brought death, the mandate was: go into cities and there will be no poor among you. We already walk in that Kingdom inheritance—and we carry the extra oomph of the new covenant. What if the homeless were drawn to your city because they knew there was hope there? Not just because of the shelters and people who care, but because hope has been restored and people wandering in desert places were made whole.

The Kingdom is the restoration of all things. It is my hope that the five-fold, too will be restored—that it will operate in authentic, healthy, relationship to bring the Kingdom. Let's repent—change our thinking—for the Kingdom is at hand.

It's all about the King and the Kingdom.

# 10: A PRAYER FOR THE FIVE-FOLD

Father, we thank you for what you've done, what you're doing, and what you're about to do. We honor the past and bless you for all that has gone before. We bless those who came before us and made a way for us. We pray for an anointing to see your Kingdom come in greater measure.

We invite you to continue building what you've been building. We are asking for more Kingdom: let it come. Let your will be done on earth as it is in Heaven. In our region as it is in Heaven.

We pray for an increased understanding of authority, of what it looks like to be a man or woman submitted to a man or woman who is submitted to God. We acknowledge that Jesus gave us all authority to cast out every demon and heal every disease.

We call for the full anointing of the five-fold and the courage to say: all things are possible. It is possible for us to get over our hurt. It is possible for us to move past the barriers in our lives. It is possible for us to do everything we are called to do.

We pray for the boldness and authority of the apostles to rise up. We pray for the prophets to shift our mindsets and lead a forthtelling generation. We pray for evangelists to bring in and clean up the lost. We pray for pastors who help heal and nurture. We pray for teachers who equipping us in truth. We pray for all the five-fold who help us to do the works of ministry.

Teach us how to run together in honor. Let your Kingdom come.

Amen.

**Q:** Can you define an apostle?

**A:** One of the groups in our school came up with an exceptional definition: "Apostles are a gift from Jesus to the Church, called in grace to build it up and equip the saints for the work of ministry, including the raising up of the five-fold. They help establish unity in the body, have a passion to see the Church grow in strength and beauty and full maturity. They actively flow in the supernatural to shift mindsets that release Heaven on earth."

Another favorite from a young guy David Toussaint in Quebec: "Apostles are sent by the Church, graced with authority to lay a foundation for the Church to be equipped to advance His Kingdom on earth. They serve by equipping the Church, stimulating gifting and callings, training leaders, teaching, and demonstrating the power of God."

**Q:** You've mentioned how young the apostles were, and I often hear older apostles calling out young people. Is there a place for older people to step out into this?

**A:** I'll answer this with Acts 2; it's time for young people to prophesy and old people to dream dreams. The absence of dreaming is the problem for my generation and older. Let's dream new dreams! We've been believing the lie that if we have a desire in our hearts, we need to die to it. No! I don't give my children a gift and then tell them: "I want you to destroy it." Imagine I give my child a car and then tell her to go crash it. No! I want her to drive the car, enjoy it. God is telling us to enjoy the gifts He gives us. Dream dreams. You're released to dream dreams.

This move of God that we have been in since Pentecost is a multi-generational move that is not about "the next generation". We need old and young five-fold leaders who are healthy, secure and moving in greater authority than ever.

**Q:** You mentioned that apostles are sent, but if we have an apostle in our church and they're not going anywhere, how are they are an apostle?

**A:** If a church has commissioned an apostle, laid hands on her, and sent her, she is sent. Sent doesn't mean you're going to leave, it just means you've been sent into your calling. Her metron will expand. Paul's prayer is that our metrons will expand.

I would fully expect that as she grows in her grace that influence and impact will expand, just let's give time to grow and develop, to become the person she is called to be.

**Q:** You've said you think we'll begin to transition from everybody being called a pastor to growing into the five-fold. I'm curious how that plays out when we gather together on Sunday or whenever we meet...what does it look like to have all of the five-fold present and working together?

**A:** The five-fold is not church governance. When we hear "five-fold" we still tend to think of government and structure. Here's a question: who is the worship leader for Sunday morning? The person up on the stage with the guitar or keyboard is not the worship leader. If I'm leading the church, I'm the worship leader. I can pause the worship time and call on the prophets to give words. The musician on the stage isn't going to say, "no." Because I'm the leader. That's how it functions.

The very simplest definition of submission is understanding who has authority. The five-fold all submit to whoever's in charge, otherwise, it's abusive. Danny Silk has a picture of five horses running together; it's a great picture of the five-fold. They all run together, and sometimes one needs to take the lead.

Local churches are led by an elder or overseer, they are the ones with the authority for their house. They are most likely not a five-fold equipper. They are probably an administrator, or a leader, or someone with a mercy gift. When the five-fold is operating, that leader will draw on and from the grace that he or she needs at that time.

**Q:** Several times in Acts, Paul describes the apostles manifesting signs and wonders and miracles. I know that this should be going on in all of our lives, but should it be going on in much greater measure in the apostles?

**A:** Yes, we should all be walking in signs, and wonders, and miracles. The confusion arises when we think there should be "super miracles."

The Apostle Paul sarcastically talked about super-apostles—there are no super-apostles. There are no super miracles. There is no super- supernatural. There are signs, miracles, wonders, and greater works. I hope everyone will move in those things; that's part of being apostolic in the truest form.

Acts 19 describes Paul doing extraordinary miracles. But the word "miracles" there isn't actually miracles. It's the word *dunamis.* So, it's not extraordinary miracles but extraordinary power. In the Corinthians' list of gifts, what is translated as the gift of miracles is actually the gift of *dunamis*: the gift of power. That's what all the mystical-realm stuff is: it's the gift of power. It's people experiencing the Spirit realm. Of course, as a bit of a mystic, I could easily try to make my definition of an apostle someone who looks like me but that wouldn't be accurate. Instead, I would say that someone who says they are an apostle and ISN'T moving in miracles, signs, and wonders is maybe not an apostle. In other words, we should all be moving in these things, and if an apostle isn't, then they maybe aren't an apostle.

I would also add that if a church is drawing from an apostle, there should be a marked growth in the manifestation of these signs, wonders, and miracles.

**Q:** I feel that so many of the five-fold are walking around with authority, but they aren't part of a local church. How does that work?

**A:** God is ridiculously good. He will still give a measure of the grace, even if the person does not walk it out as it should be walked out. That person will experience blessing, impact, and influence. However, if they were to walk in the grace as I think it should, then all that they currently walk in will be multiplied and God's favor will be added.

Think of it in terms of seeing hundreds impacted versus seeing thousand impacted. The Kingdom is about increase and my expectation is that once properly aligned, their impact will multiply a hundred-fold.

**Q:** Could someone be an apostle if they are sent by a church to start a business that can reduce poverty and bring people into wealth?

**A:** I think if you're called to start businesses, you should be a businessperson. Don't worry about being an apostle; you don't need to be an apostle to start a business. In fact, I'd say it would confuse things. Just do one thing and do it really well. Start those businesses that get people out of poverty. Do that. That's Kingdom.

Apostles are called to the Church. They're not called to the marketplace.

**Q:** If someone has an entrepreneurial gifting and they want to use it with Kingdom principles and mindset and wants to equip others with that, and that is their metron, is it possible that someone can be an apostle with a marketplace metron?

**A:** Doubtful. There is no biblical model. Are there marketplace pastors? Marketplace teachers? Marketplace evangelists? Nobody seems to want to be a marketplace evangelist.

They all want to be marketplace apostles. It's just apostles because we think apostles are at the top of the ladder, and maybe it's just that we want to be at the top of the ladder. We misinterpret "first of all, apostles." Remember, it's not about rank or status. That Scripture is about chronology: first we do this, then we do this, and lastly this." But if it's about rank, who wants to be number two? We all want to be number one. I suspect that rank and status is largely the motivation of calling people marketplace apostles.

We also forget that the five-fold operate together. So, if you claim to have a marketplace apostle, who's their connected prophet, evangelist, pastor, and teacher—and how are they running with the other five-fold? Instead of trying to raise up a five-fold entrepreneur, just be a really good Kingdom entrepreneur. Make billions of dollars, train other people to make billions of dollars. You don't need a Christianese label.

**Q:** What is the conversation churches need to be having about the five-fold now that they're not having?

**A:** I don't think I'm interested in churches having a conversation, but I am interested in gathering the emerging apostles and figuring out what we are going to build. That's the conversation I'm interested in. I don't feel called to convince people; I feel called to build something. Nothing will stir up the hearts of men and women as building something.

For years, I worked in Northern Ireland trying to get Protestants and Catholics to not kill each other—quite literally not kill each other. I understand conflict, and I understand trying to convince people of the right thing. But nothing works better than show and tell: to show, "This is what we're building—join us in building up the Kingdom. "Seek first the Kingdom, and all these things will be added to you."

**Q:** Why do so many evangelists have a reputation for hating the Church?

**A:** All the five-fold are called to the Church. They're equipping the saints to minister. You can't really be called to the Church and hate the Church. That's a bit of dodgy thinking.

What we have seen are unhealthy evangelists. These are the ones saying, "The Church is a hateful organization that just hurts people—and why are we even spending money on buildings anyway? Why are we having a capital campaign when people are going to hell? Heck! We could buy twenty churches in Africa for the price of this one church." That's unhealthy. Evangelists love the church and are called to equip her.

**Q:** Is there a difference between the gift of evangelism and the gift of the evangelist?

A: We mistakenly think evangelists "do" evangelism. Where do we get that from? We're making it up. I can find no gift of evangelism in scripture.

We have a tendency to confuse Romans 12, I Corinthians 12, and Ephesians 4. Here's my assumption: the gifts in Romans 12 and I Corinthians 12 are abilities. Stuff that we can do. You can receive them through the laying on of hands, you can ask for them, have them imparted, etc. But the Ephesians 4 gifts are not abilities. They are people. The gifts of Jesus are people.

I have a credit card I love. I get so many perks with it—it's fantastic. Upgrades here, there, and everywhere. As an itinerant traveler, it's a phenomenal credit card to have. I've just become an evangelist for that credit card; I believe that it makes a difference in my life, and I'm going to tell everyone about it. This thing has brought my life good, therefore, I'm going to tell everyone.

The role of the evangelist isn't so much about bringing people to Jesus as about bringing Jesus to people. Remember: there is no gospel of salvation in Scripture, it is the Gospel of the Kingdom.

The evangelist is fanatical about the Kingdom. They go all over, saying, "Let me introduce you to the King! Let me tell you what He's done in my life." To do that you need to have experienced the goodness of the Kingdom yourself. It's wildly different thinking from standing on a street corner, holding up a sign saying the rapture is going to come; that's not really good news. That's not the gospel of the Kingdom. The gospel of the Kingdom is that the Kingdom has come, and the Kingdom is coming. Jesus is King and will change your life for the better of you let Him.

**Q:** Is it possible that malfunctions in the five-fold occur when they are operating in their strength but not actually being supported in the way they need to be? Might the dysfunctions be a clue into these roles? And why do you think these five are the five? Why doesn't an administrator get on the list of five-fold, for instance?

**A:** Anything's possible. Instead of possible, I go for probable. If I hear hooves, I hear horses, not zebras. So, I think it's more probable that people don't understand how submission to authority works. In my experience, it's not about a misunderstood five-fold as it is about a frustrated or angry or bitter person who doesn't understand submission. I know that's not very popular, but I used to wear a uniform, and I understand how authority works.

I also think there are misunderstandings of how governance works in the Church. I don't believe that the Ephesians 4 description of the five-fold refers to governance offices. And I don't believe that every church needs a five-fold team; that's actually a really bad idea because you just start appointing people who aren't five-fold. I do think every church needs to be connected with an apostle and prophet, and I think part of the role of an apostle and prophet will be to reproduce themselves, but they're not the governance.

The overseer of the church is the overseer of the church—whether you call them a senior pastor, senior leader, elder, whatever. The five-fold have a role in correcting and aligning. Understanding authority is really important. I actually have the Greek word for authority tattooed on my arm because it's what the five-fold is about.

And you ask why these five? These five have access to an authority—particularly the apostle and then the prophet—that the rest of the gifts need to pull on. That's probably one of the biggest issues in the Church: the absence of authority or the absence of understanding authority.

Jesus gave these gifts to rule and He rules by love, service, and submitting to His father.

**Q:** Can you give more examples of a five-fold teacher?

**A:** A five-fold teacher brings truth that advances the Kingdom. All five-fold should have the Romans 12 gift of teaching; like any leader or authority in the Church, they should be "apt to teach," as the old King James English phrased it.

The five-fold teacher brings revelation from Scripture. Anointed teachers bring a fresh revelation that expands our view of the Kingdom. We probably all remember the first time we read Bill Johnson's book *When Heaven Invades Earth*. And if you're like me, you read a page and then put it down just to take it in, because it messes with you in a good way; it's all about renewing our minds—changing our thinking. That's the kind of revelation we expect from a five-fold teacher. It's not just about teaching people how to raise their families and do their finances; that's Romans 12. The five-fold teacher will bring a revelatory spin to everything we've read.

I've also been listening to Brian Simmons talking about being one with God. My mind is blown because of this five-fold teacher bringing a depth of revelation that is changing my experience of the Kingdom.

**Q:** We've been told you have to be recognized by another prophet to be a prophet, recognized by an apostle to be an apostle, etc. How do you recognize these gifts?

**A:** In the Bible, we see the local church in Antioch recognizing that Paul and Barnabas had become apostles; they laid hands on them. That's it. So, for me, it's the local church that needs to recognize an apostle under the guidance of the Holy Spirit. And to do that, they need to understand what an apostle is, or a prophet, or an evangelist, or a pastor, or a teacher. I can't go to a church in Texas and tell them who their apostles are. It's supposed to be done organically, relationally.

I think the five-fold person needs an inner conviction, and I think people in authority need to see and acknowledge it.

People don't "become" apostles or prophets, it isn't a promotion. It is a grace given by God that is recognized by the leaders of a local church who lay hands on the person and commission them.

**Q:** In Acts 6: 4, the twelve apostles say will devote themselves to prayer and the ministry of the Word. When I look at Bill Johnson or Heidi Baker, that seems like one of the dominant parts of who they are—their devotion to prayer and the presence of the Lord. I'd like you to comment on the role of that when you see apostolic people. Do you see that as a dominant trait in their life?

**A:** The healthy answer is yes. We want to raise up healthy apostles and prophets. But there are some unhealthy ones out there, too. Just because they're unhealthy doesn't mean they're not apostles and prophets. In addition to devoting themselves to prayer and the Word, they also need to be in submission to someone—to have someone adjusting and correcting them. I think we should all be like that.

# FINAL ADVICE TO CHURCH LEADERS

There is a bit of confusion over the role of father/mother and apostle. At the outset, I would suggest that an apostle is not a father/mother but then again, they may be. Every father/mother is also not an apostle, but again, they may be. One is a specific grace (apostle), the other is a role (father/mother) and they have been confused, largely in my opinion, because of the reluctance in some parts of the church to recognize apostles, preferring the term father/mother instead.

The problem is that everyone should be a father/mother and demonstrate the heart of our Good, Good, Father but not everyone is an apostle. You may have a father/mother in your life and the life of your church, that does not mean you have an apostle.

The fact you have this in your hands means there is a good chance I do not need to convince you of the basic need for a church to have an apostle, one who is outside the leadership of the church. In case I do, let me suggest that a large reason 85% of seminary graduates who enter ministry will drop out in a couple of years is that they do not have the grace for frontline warfare, the very grace that apostles carry.

Apostles are not necessarily the leaders of a local church, they are a resource for the local church. At times you will find the leader of a local church who walks in the grace of an apostle. In my experience, that leader will always have a vision larger than their local church and will have influence beyond their own congregation. Even if the local church has an apostle as their leader, I believe the Biblical pattern is to maintain a relationship with another apostle.

In 1 Corinthians 4 where Paul is describing apostolic ministry, he says "So then you must perceive us—*not as leaders of factions*, but as servants of the Anointed One, those who have been entrusted with God's mysteries."

Brian Simmons describes the word "servants" this way in his footnotes on 1 Corinthians 4 in The Passion Translation this way:

*"Paul uses an unusual Greek word, huperetes, which means "subordinate" or "personal assistant." The compound word huperetes literally means "under-rowers," and it is used in classical Greek to describe those who sit on benches in the*

*lower parts of the ship rowing. Apostolic ministry does not mean that an apostle is seen as important and in first place, but as one who will often be in a hidden role of moving a church and region forward as a subordinate of our captain, Jesus Christ."*

I couldn't have put it better myself!

In my opinion, every church leader should get their church an *under-rower*. But what does that mean? What does it look like to have an apostle? I have been asked that but have not answered it really well so here are some of my thoughts.

## Build

Please do not enter a long-term commitment with an apostle because they demand it or because they are an attractive option. Pray and build a relationship with each other. Really, it is a lot like dating. Yep, you heard me, date your prospective apostle. Make sure there is chemistry, that you actually like the guy or gal and enjoy having a meal with him or her. Make sure your spouse (if you have one) likes them as well. Even make sure you like the potential apostle's spouse. And make sure that you are experiencing their grace. If they carry courage, you should feel braver around them. If they carry hope, you should feel more hopeful around them. Not only around them but it should be a deposit they leave with you. Make sure your prospective apostle meets your staff, your leaders, your board. You are not looking for consensus, you are simply introducing this new significant person in your life to those already present.

Once you have both decided it is a good fit, then comes the relational piece. Learning to ask questions, draw from the apostle in many matters, is vital. Just remember it is the apostolic grace you are drawing from, not the pastoral or teacher. It is the grace to be strong and courageous, to build, and to bring unity which in my experience is often about sniffing our disunity and misalignment.

**Sow**

If you have an apostle, you should sow into them each month. I am thankful that it was the apostle Paul who said in 1 Corinthians 9 in The Passion Translation,

> So, to those who want to continually criticize my apostolic ministry, here's my statement of defense. Don't we apostles have the right to be supported financially? Don't we have the right to travel accompanied by our believing wives and be supported as a couple?

He then went on to draw a direct relationship with the terumah or first fruits given to the priests and his apostolic ministry.

> Don't you know that the priests employed
> in sacred duty in the temple are provided
> for by temple resources? And the priests
> who serve at the altar receive a portion of
> the offerings? In the same way, the Lord has
> directed those who proclaim the gospel to
> receive their living by the gospel.

I love that Paul uses the phrase "in the same way" which I interpret not only the principle of paying a wage but also where it comes from, i.e. the first fruit or terumah.

### Draw

I also think that if you have an apostle, you should draw from them regularly, use their strength and authority as your covering, and at least once a year bring them into your body to make a strategic deposit that helps you build what you are building. Learn how to draw from their grace. Learn how to not only talk but draw from their grace. That may differ from apostle to apostle and church to church, but this is a long-term investment and one that is worth it but ultimately, every apostle should impart the grace to be obedient to what you have been called to do. There will be an impartation of courage, of believing you can do what He has called you to do, and ultimately hope.

I actually believe that it should be the apostle that sets the senior leader's salary and benefits. It removes it from history, petty politics, and also from "pastoral humility" that can plague a senior leader.

I would strongly encourage each leader of a local church to have an apostle outside of their local body, someone you can draw from, and that can help you build. Make sure it is someone you have chemistry with, someone you actually like and please, let it be someone who really is an apostle! If you need help finding one, let me know.

# ABOUT THE AUTHOR

Ian Carroll has as a vision to see people, churches, and ministries encouraged and strengthened to become the world-changers they were born to be. He and his wife, Rachel, serve local churches as their apostle and/or prophet, they equip emerging apostles and prophets, and they minister to the body. For more information, visit, www.building-contenders.com